MW00935543

A BIG Thank You for a Wonderful Year.

with love from:

WORKPLACE WONDERS

This notebook belongs to

Made in the USA
Middletown, DE
13 June 2024

55734073R00066